DESIGN FAULT

In loving memory of my mother
Brenda Agnes Natzler (1915–2000)
who gave me everything

Also by Caroline Natzler

FICTION
Water Wings
(Onlywomen Press 1990)

POETRY
Speaking the Wetlands
(Pikestaff 1998)

DESIGN FAULT

Caroline Natzler

Jean - Christophe
Best wishes
Carrie

FLAMBARD

ACKNOWLEDGEMENTS

Some of these poems have appeared in the following magazines:
Equinox, The Frogmore Papers, Magma, Nineties Poetry,
Other Poetry, Poetry London, Poetry Wales, Seam, Smith's Knoll,
Staple, Tears in the Fence, The Wide Skirt, and *Writing Women;*
also in two anthologies published by Oscars Press:
Of Eros and of Dust and *As Girls Could Boast;*
in *Parents*, an anthology from Enitharmon;
in the *Big Wide Words* exhibition on London buses;
and in the author's pamphlet collection:
Speaking the Wetlands (Pikestaff, 1998).

First published in England in 2001 by Flambard Press
Stable Cottage, East Fourstones, Hexham NE47 5DX

Typeset by Harry Novak
Cover design by Gainford Design Associates
Printed in England by Cromwell Press, Trowbridge, Wiltshire

A CIP catalogue record for this book
is available from the British Library.

ISBN 1 873226 42 X

Flambard Press wishes to thank Northern Arts
for its financial support.

Website: www.flambardpress.co.uk

CONTENTS

Design Fault

How come there are still design faults
in things as normal as toasters?
Not a new device, edgy with the hubris of invention.
My grandmother had one. A grilled mouse
slid up over the rim one morning
sudden and flat as a stunt gone wrong.

I wake in the night sometimes, in pieces
– I'm darkness, choking –

Quite normal, people say, this fear.
Look after yourself, make yourself some toast.

Can one cook up comfort for oneself
must it not be given?

My old toaster wouldn't switch off.
The elements went on burning, manic
until it shot into flames and caved in on itself
melting into folds of bruised, lumpen matter.

But the new one is cool to the touch, long as a smile,
gleaming with savoir-faire
even in the critical glare of the kitchen light
at this wrong time.
Inside, the elements are intricate
like bits of writing, or music.
They work to electronic timings till the toast is perfect.
It jolts up –
one slice tossed behind the unit
where there's only dust and lost things –
the next flat on the cold white floor
final as a lid.
The spring's too violent.

I open the curtains to numb dark shapes
open them wide to make the morning come,
trust it will.

Marking the Waste

Bone-bare, and restless.

Something missing
dumb as a hole in the heart.

Something you should be doing, surely?
The surging, the deep tidal pull of it
soughing always back into silence.

No clue on this stretch of white earth.

Is it enough that your ragged shadow
marking the waste for a moment
doubles you,
brushing a lucid, fleeting pictogram?
That your cry calls an echo?

Life Span

Only I in my place feel the touch of the sun.
Only I can turn my kaleidoscope
blinking at the mosaic of centuries,
the world wheeling only within my horizon.

Yet I clamber in and out of garments, bracing
against monumental cold,
against bloody explosion.

My path is strewn with seeds and crackling leaves.
Indoors I tread lightly
not to crush red berries deep
into the terra cotta carpet, which to me is golden.

Absence

It was only something vanished
no sure name, and never quite held to.
Yet through the years
through the making-do hours and days
came the pull

a straining in the air
a longing at the brink of things

as if to lift

but she weighed low,
stranded.

Only the pull at her bones
angling her elsewhere

only her taut mind
tensed

for a word floating to the floor
in script she cannot read
slipping like the print from a dream

or a rush of light at the door.

The Scientist's Brain, the Explorer's Shoe and the Sleeping Beauty

Inspired by 'The Maybe' by Tilda Swinton and Cornelia Parker, Serpentine Gallery, June–September 1995

The Great Scientist's brain floats in formaldehyde
like an embryo
knotted with grey swellings.
The Great Explorer's left shoe lies sloughed off
on a cushion, the leather flaking.
A young woman in a nightie sleeps in a perspex case.
A glass of water trembles in the corner.

Most of the time you just get on with things, don't you?
– Taking in the milk bottles every morning
clutching your dressing gown close
wondering what would happen if one day it fell open
– Making lists, switching things around
piecing them together, crossing things off
– Treading the earth till your sole's bald
shooing the cat out at night.

Who decides when something's Happened?
That your life, all the gettings up and goings to bed
and the shuffling bits inbetween,
is charged with grace
everything geared to one glorious Moment?

Really I hardly noticed his kiss, it was raining so hard
and the front garden was full of sparrow noise,
though after he moved in it's true
the milk started coming in cartons
so you don't have to worry about the birds
pecking at the gold tops.
All the milk for us.

But the lists still need to be done
and you don't stop thinking
whether you've done the right thing, whether you deserve it
how it hangs together, how to keep it all going

and once your sole's too bruised to go on
your laces are knotted up and you're lying curled
in a glass case with a label beside you

you'll wonder if whoever wrote that epitaph
really had a clue.

Why I Get Angry

At the ending of a day
quilted in sea and silky air
ribboned with cliff-top walks, lifting blue
and fringed with sand sifting between my toes,
a day stitched into meaning by the sureness of friends
and embroidered with bright fantasies of thought
peace touching my limbs with velvet,
I lash out
let rip at any pinprick nuisance
tear shreds off some stranger
spit cutting words at toddlers and doe-eyed dogs,
swear, my body raddled with rage,
hate myself for it
– and all to scratch out the impossible sheen of happiness
unpick the perfect, glowing fabric
like the old weaver knotting a tactful flaw
in every prayer rug;
and to pre-empt the fraying of time,
tomorrow's ragged grey.
So I sleep safe in familiar edginess
and the guilt that is close to my soul
as dirt under fingernails,
my sheets ruckled, my pillow bumpy.

Thus

1. There shall be grey snow melt water

2. Any dark conical thing must be wedged
   in grey snow melt water or slush

3. Snow melt water shall drift under the sky
   the sky shall be hazy

4. Any dark conical thing must be ridged

5. There shall be a circle of dark water around
   the bottom of the dark conical thing
   in the grey snow melt water or slush

6. There shall be loose water
   there shall be water meandering into the middle distance
   there shall be bleak grey mush or slush

7. The dark conical thing may be an unexploded bomb
   The dark conical thing may be a water hydrant
   The dark conical thing may be a bollard
   The dark conical thing may be an object of worship
   at prescribed hours

8. Any shed house or other dwelling
   situated behind and to the left
   of the dark conical thing
   shall be divided from the said dark conical thing
   by loose meandering water

9. Any such shed as aforesaid
   shall be brownish red

10. The sun may lighten the Eastern corner
    of the brownish red shed
    the sun may reflect the shed in the water but any
    such reflection must be divided from the shed
    by a ledge of the snow melt slush

Picnic, Llyn Peninsula, 1902

'Father, I must whisper this.'
High on the cliff.

'Father, I must whisper this.' Or
the wind will snatch, shriek –
black rocks and gulls and the standing stone tilted
to the edge will hear
and make this real.

'Father, I must whisper this.'
So it does not count
it is not quite done
and the crashing sea for a hush of time
may hang
a moment when you can still say, Please
may it not have happened.

'Father, I must whisper this.'

Pastoral

If only a milk jug, a bowl of rosy apples
even a nursery cock ablaze with angry feathers…
she could deal with cows being murdered
in the low field
wind rustling flakes of earth under the door.
A time when you could fasten
to the tick of the grandfather clock.

But this, an eclipse of the sun on TV
a squeal of brakes in the street outside.

Always That Cry

That cry in your mind – Mother! –
only it's not. Just a gasp,
releasing. You hug the air
hold fast to the triangle of light
shivering at the top of the curtains.

That cry in your mind – God! –
only it's not.
A spasm in the dark.
You listen for the dense chatter of the airwaves, and friends
calling long distance.

That whisper in your mind:
Don't walk through the long evening grass
with your shadow pulling ahead
rocking over the bristling seeds. Stop
before your head reaches the bare road.
Turn, turn and face the sun,
you've seen the sun go down before.

And now, seeing your shadow on a golden tree,
upright, coming towards you.

Interior

Not glass it seems in this yellowing window
laid into marble walls,
only a flayed skin hanging
bare and jaundiced,
only as much sour light as the skin lets in
to the throne room,
and at the centre the sacred flame
snapping and pricking
against a clutch of soot.

To the scientist who showed me

complexity
a regular beat the sign of a diseased heart
but so alive the crazy heart awakened leap

how birds are aerodynamically unstable
attentive to air
each flutter an uncertain
communion, which may become a journey

how proteins fold close
touching as many surfaces as possible
in a warm interplay of hints and cues
our livelong process

how life may have evolved in the deep heave
of oceans unsounded by sunlight
in extremity
deliciousness squeezing into being
in the dark flow

and how you
my becoming world
(o my universe!)
come belling through my new flushed life
this astonished emptiness

come resounding through
and all is flow

Knowledge of the Universe

'Physics is almost complete,' you say
sipping the exact, sharp water you call seltzer,
telling me all you know, dancing for me
years since we were students.
I'm jet-lagged.
We sit on your steel deck. Steamy air
that clings to the skin like a lover.
A jumble of air conditioners
Pandora's boxes crouching on window sills
belching out hot indoor smells,
overhead wires, tall trees with dim leaves,
purple morning glory brazen as lipstick,
the frantic turns of fire escapes, tight bird sounds,
shouts from nowhere and always
the New York counterpoint of sirens,
endless suck and cry.

'Physics will soon be finished. Isn't that wonderful to think?
All done.'
You smile, stretch your legs.
Your mock-pearls perfect, lily white, heavy on your chest.
'The universe is limitless but finite.
Nothing for God to do.'

Driving from the airport I saw washing slung out
on long aching pulleys between apartment blocks,
a child's tee-shirt
high up, buffeted in the hound-hot wind from the motorway
flapping in the space between buildings.
Perhaps, I thought, it will be pulled back inside soon
worn a day on a proud chest
washed, mangled, slung out again into the raging air.

'Everything is determined.
In principle everything is predictable
though not all the equations are quite worked out yet.'
You glance at me – teasing?
I never quite know the steps of your dance.

You've been listening to popular-science tapes.
'Nothing else to do on the subway to work.'
The seltzer spits with light.
'Space isn't empty. It ripples.'
The bubbles dissolve on the tongue.

In every gritty corner of the world, I think
Sisyphus goes on pushing his rock up the mountain
through scrub, thorn bushes
and stones, deep shadowed like skulls.

For Cathy

Out of Earth

Animal limbs ripple, thousands of years old
blood dark, fleeting
into shadows and bulges of rock
snuffling, stampeding life
drawn deep in.

When faces appear in her living-room floor
then disappear
and everyone in the village sees,
she's told; it is nothing.
Just the days and changes of earth
under concrete.

At the mouth of the cave
sits a row of silent babies
slow-eyed, in dumpling white nappies
fed, cleaned, sheltered

and somewhere, in a red and golden gallery
lifted on slender columns
a child ululates into the air.

A Northerner's Metaphysics

On a beach of hot white stones
you might not think
life is like a dog lead hanging in a cold hall.

You might lie in the sun like Cleopatra.

Your fingers might play the piano
adrift in the air, sun-reflecting nails
drawn up and down on threads of light.

Grazing the stones your fingernail might snag
on the carcass of a frizzled bee, zigzagged down
from the mulberry trees on the lower slopes.
You might bury it under round stones.

The sun's heat might crown your head
as you squint at old markings
etched into the stones.

You might throw stones,
not like a person launching rockets or sowing seeds
– but simply to watch them vanish
soundless into the surf.

Lying regal under the dome of sky
you might hear the waters roar in
hesitate
swish back to the pull of the moon.

You might not think
life is like a blue plastic bucket
waiting for a drip from the ceiling.

Hyperactivity

This yet another day in life
knots of energy, configurations
of information, the blurry
sighting of a planet beyond
our solar system, fifty light years away
gaseous, no solid surfaces for life
yet blue-green, like Earth.

No word
from anywhere.

I finger my pen
look out through glass, watch
birds growing frantic with light
leaves flipping sunlight into shadow.

Reach

Still so far, the sky
blue receding of our longing
clouds that may unfurl
reveal

though we've sat up there tight-packed
passing the time, watching the plane's shadow
cross the clouds below
and silence all around is riddled
with us, techno-vibrant with our calls

only something is bounded
– the break in the voice
ache in the tapping fingertips –
unable, quite, to reach.

Through the Years

Deep in the library the scholar picks at her spots
till blood drips, smearing over the book's tight print
and the years press pale against the window pane.
If she studies long enough she may attain the honour
of seeing the Emperor dying.

The company commissions a thousand golden cages
for its Millennium girls.

The revolutionary beats down the studded doors
blows bubbles at the grey assembled heads
– 'End the system!' –
proud that her younger sisters will surely
see the Emperor die.

Millennium computers swoon at the trail of open 000's.

In a palace of sublime light
the mystic beholds her Emperor dying,
aghast that she, her body self, survives
knees sore, fingernails bitten to the quick.

The company donates a thousand golden rocks
to Millennium Project Sisyphus.

The worker hunches, clicking through the long glowing night
earns a coffee mug inscribed in gilt
'The Emperor is dead, long live the Emperor!'

The company patents ten thousand dragons
to patrol Millennium children.

The old turner of the world,
tall-headed, squatting flesh
scrabbles in the taps of the earth
roots out buried golden bulbs

gives birth in the hugeness between her legs
rises, stretches, picks her teeth
and rocks the Emperor in his winding sheet.

The company sells tickets to see the sun's eclipse
at the end of the land.

Nurture

Pull out the ancestors
with their deep open mouths round as harmony
their horns, animal faces, sturdy human bodies
bearing the holy things,
and their garments webbed with wind
fired with the colours of earth
the bend of sky on their feathers.

Pull out the ancestors
from the warmth of your armpits
your pockets, your hair
the faded box that's always been there
the places you played as a child.
Against the whisperings of your aunts
take them elsewhere.

Sell your ancestor dolls
to the cultural museum
to pay for your college fees

become like the slim white girls
nibbling at small effigies of themselves.

Outside the Museum

In the old places
the trance of stones
circling cold fields,
Mayan temples grimly stepped
to the sky

    here a young woman arches her neck, bare
    to the street wind, lets her hair sway

certain slants of stone
or tunnelled light shafts
are finely aligned

    how she walks –
    the tune of her long legs –
    how she relishes

to where the sun sets at the equinoxes
when the veil is thin

    moving as if she were the first
    as if there'd been no beauty, love
    we might long to remember

those worn stones, temples for sacrifice
for the release of souls into stars

    she smiles

    the world goes on making this new.

Gravity

What do the men in helmets think
striding past me with their sealed packages?

Do they see a woman with dust in her hair
hovering at a door which doesn't say Psychotherapist
though everyone in the building must know?
Battersea Business Centre, thin, sick corridors
where the air drains me of breath.
I can slip away, I don't have to be here.

They tread past, steaming slightly in their black bike gear
absorbed in the work of the world
vizors jacked up, chin guards jutting.
A nose like a drugged laboratory animal
exposed.
Eyes counting, looking for room numbers.

I don't want her to open the door.
The soft blonde smile that opens to chaos
a blur-of plants, white threads drifting from the cushions
and behind my eyes, the shredding.

Stay with the work of the world.

The men's boots are so big, clumpy
– space boots, giants' clogs, a child in his father's shoes –
as if they feared loss of gravity
weightlessness.

Biographical Notes

'Her life's preoccupation was how to represent
solid objects on a flat surface.'

Why?
Could this woman not live replete
in the roundness of the real?

Dr Johnson kicked a stone and said,
There's an end to it; the world exists.
He kept iron shackles in case he went mad.

Maybe the artist meant to work magic
release her too solid world
into some realm beyond
the cramping curve of space and time,
though she could only move things around,
level onto the grey weave of the canvas
the belly of a vase
white petals shrinking brown at the edges
dust lying soft as a veil.

Nothing goes beyond what we can know
and we can only move things around,
meeting no god – neither on the moon
nor folded in the darkness of outer space.
Nothing beyond the shadowless
men and women who walk there,
float there.

For What?

Words slither
like the decoy eyes of fish tails.

No straight answer.

Every dogged alarm clock day
blocks the way with rubbish.

Wind in the hair on the corniche road
only stirs dull blood and oxygen.

Scribble away the years of life
waiting for the angel.

Waiting

I bobbed in a birdcage on a milky sea
lapping at the skyline until
the bars splintered like icicles
and in tears I rose, climbed hard stairs
to work, sat straight at the desk,
pecked at by eye-scratching print.
I called my mother who was waiting for a funeral.
'A green December fills the graves,' she said.
I heard the tapping of her broken fingernails
and yanked away the cord.
Then all was quiet, the grey phone hung loose as bone
and all day I watched the sky reverse
the clouds pull back
and wondered if I would ever see my home.

There

She's there in the way you mark a cross
with the point of a knife
on the bleak roots of the sprouts.
In the way you roll your thumbs in silence
through the long evening.

The boiler throbs in her warm kitchen
where the field mice scrabble at night
and the household dog quivers in dream.
She's there.
Her earth-green apron levels the mounds of her body
and the swollen tea cosy waits on the table
in the place where you ate the gingerbread men
head first, better that than the gradual nibbling at the limbs.

She's there in the way you walk
fixing your gaze to the grid of the pavement,
in the way your chin wobbles when you will not cry.

There in the garden where through the slats in the fence
you can just glimpse the shimmering girl in pink
the forbidden girl, whose mother keeps chickens,
whose father flings swear words into the slow afternoon.
She's there with you
knitting in the shade, watching you dig deep in the sandpit
deep enough to get right in.

In the chill in your stomach at the calling of your name
she's there. In the snarling of your thoughts
at the touch of skin soft words.

Behind the housefront crossed with painted beams
and the windows blocked with the backs of mirrors
she's there.

On the front door a red glass tulip lifts like a chalice
and down the hall where the carpet strains
between black stained boards
she's there.
And there's a long chain on the lavatory pull
and a heaving and a heartbeat silence
before the wedding-dress frothing of the water.

In the house where one icy afternoon
she brought in clothes from the line
rigid with frost.
Look! she laughed, showing her teeth. See!

How the trousers stood up on end
and the dress was hollow.

Holiday

In France, in the stunned midday heat
when my mother slept
my brother and I watched a lizard
nosing out from under a rock
tensing its baby fingers on the road
to dart into sunlight.
My father came along in our new black Ford
and ran it over, by mistake.
We crouched beside it
touched the creature's nobbly back,
colours of petrol spilled in a puddle.
Its delicate feet were spoiled
like scribbles.
I held my tongue between my teeth
then told my brother to stop sniffling.

Later we played Dead Lizards
lying beside each other on the nursery floor.

1955

Hitler and Mussolini shrieking on a lawn so green
it can only exist in memory,
chasing each other round and round
sheer as our dog's early morning frenzy.
Mussolini was the one who was fat
so my little brother had to arch his back
to stick his tummy out
slowing him almost into my breathless clutches
as I charged after him in lace-up shoes
squelching moisture from the grass
my red pleated skirt flapping
like wind-crazed flags against my legs.
'Hitler and Mussolini! Hitler and Mussolini!'
pealing into the still air
– oh yes! –
and my father deep behind his newspaper
in the shade, keeping silent.

Several Make a Chain

Several go to Scotland and have an adventure.
One watches a white butterfly near a white-washed wall.

Several laugh behind their hands, whisper the password.
One fixes her eyes hot on her story-book's hazy print.

Several huddle together, make plans,
link arms through the forest.
One circles her dark room, reciting words beginning with Z.

Several invent great punishments
for the good of those who break the rules.
One gazes at the slipping of light in a windy pool.

One picks a daisy, long stem hanging loose,
several make a chain, uneasy round the neck.

Just Growing Up

The swelling grey window
loomed over her,
shrank to a prick of mocking light.
No, you dreamt it.

Splinters of shell crushed into crazy paving,
stripped ivy, clawing at a wall
softened her teeth.
Hypersensitive.

Ideas tapped against her mind
hot words billowing by, glances.
In her white cardigan she felt too small.
Being precious.

She floated. Greyness bandaged
the inside of her mind.
Outside, men laughed and chewed sausages.
Perfectly normal, just growing up.

The moon hung sharp.
She saw the trains slip by
carrying the plague
sealed in the sleeping compartments.
You'll come to terms with it.

To Have Had a Youth

To have walked home in the dawn
thinking at first the rhythm of my walk
was lightening the night,
adventure and the power of blood,
or that the street lights were brightening
like spotlights swelling a stage with light and grandeur,
then to realise
it was only the yawn of a grey morning.

Girls

I'm suspicious of girls.

They come right up to you in the street
peering at you – flashing bold silver earrings
bright as knives – just to ask you the time
though there's a perfectly good clock on the Town Hall
and plenty of other mousy women to pick on.

They home in on you at the bus stop
with their black leggings and defiant crotches.
'When's the next bus to the Caley?'
'Is this the right stop for the 53?'
Obviously they're local, and know.
Their hair is all tossed with ruffled velvet bands
so close you can smell its warmth, like a nest,
but they glare at you, stud eyed.
'I don't know. 20 minutes.'
They turn away
as though nothing had happened.

All those girls in the High Street
walking as if they were the centre of the world.

I dyed my hair so I'd recognise myself in the mirror
but the roots are hazy at the parting.
Old women in buses used to give me the creeps
a chill to the stomach.
Made my fingers feel like bone.
Looking at me with pallid watery eyes
which knew too much,
slithering away, inward, indifferent.
Some weary wisdom, nothing but waste.

I stuck my tongue out yesterday, made devil fingers
at a bus driver who skimmed on by,
a young man enthroned in his warm red cabin.
Suppose I did reach out my arm too late?

Rage, scorching ripples of hate, cursing,
pierce him again and again
slice him
on a monster cheese grater
shrivel, gasp, gasp, and die.

I don't hate the girls like that.

I saw one who looked like an almost squashed beetle,
bunched up black tutu under her leather jacket
thin legs in black tights.
She looked all around as she walked
arching her neck, and she swayed
as if her body was something she was carrying
and she wavered slightly under the responsibility.

Against Amber

Afternoons ghosted with golden light
an afterglow
laying like an old woman's ringed hand
on my waiting notebook
my little gilt-framed mirror,
varnishing my broken pearls
my open sea shells,
embalming them in antique light
claiming the things of my life as relics
to pull me back to something not mine

my mother's, my mother's mother's longing
and all their important dawns.

These amber afternoons
I perch on my half-made bed
on the bare sheet,
watch the fidgeting bones
in my feet and hands,
wonder about the desert.

Adult Education: Summer School

Outside, cauled in familiar rain.
Indoors the others pass each other little cakes at long tables.
Sunken wood smells for breath
the rotting ridges of a log my centre
and for company, fingernail creatures
moulded from mud, grass and warm nose-pickings.
A child crouching in my mind's roots.
I shrink from the squelch of footsteps
the bobbing of umbrellas through the trees
and shelter in the veil of rain until they pass
bouncing back to class. The rain stops.
I stir, move an inch, crack a twig.
Outstill the rabbits
pointed in shock
like tiny churches
at the edge of the field.

No natural human empathy, what's wrong with her?

Yet I lullabied the widow
as she worried at the problem
of clipping grass round circular flower beds.
I rose flushing to the goatee beard's challenge
and shredded his philosophy of life
declining his glass of wine
and at the turn of the stairs I always smile my warmest
at the raven-haired woman from Spain
tense in her flounces, luscious as a waxed fruit,
whom everyone avoids, especially the husbands.

Crows crash among the branches
and a dog shakes something brown and limp, trots off.
I step from the trees into slender sunlight.
The field is fluffed with white feathers
souls drifting from people's mouths.

Generations

The light glares on my mirror's surface.

I see lidded brown eyes, heavy with another time,
a time glimpsed in some other mirror
lying broken in a gutter
– Warsaw or Vienna, I forget –
splinters from a door, boots,
eyes cast down on cracked glass, doubting
before they vanished.

In my mirror, tangles of hair misty at the roots
spinning into uneasy brown
that froths a defiant chemical pink
where the light shines through.
Hair that would be otherwise.

Other mirrors framed proud black hair, and grey
piled above lace and silk or a ragged shawl.
No mirror when it fell
shorn, leaving stunned nakedness.

In my mirror, a long mouth,
teeth filled with whitewash.
Weaving through the hair
a finger which won't be ringed.

Turn the mirror over.

Absolute

It laid a long straight road to the horizon
lined by sullen trees
to guard the wire fence.
Drew the sky thin.

It sought her out
and found her thinking.
Her dog lay skinny in the corner.

She chafed at the muddle of her kind
a conspiracy of chatter
choking up the emptiness,
under the cosmetics and wrinkles
the random talk and reaching out,
that space between each atom.

She sought it out.

It lasered the road bald
against the sproutings of chance.
No fuzzy dandelions, no toad ogling the day
no book someone happened to have written
dropped in the ditch.
It clipped the kerbs
defined final edges
pinched into place
each knot in the glaring fence
left the way stark.

It set her on her way
pulled the dog's bark into howling
numbed the sound of her footsteps
till she could only hear their echo.

It worked its way into her
smoothed the creases made by her breathing.
Poked her with its intelligent fingers
broke her bones into an abstract scheme.

She lay, an exact, still sign
under the shadows of the shifting clouds.
Only the dog lifted its nose to the air
wriggled under the wire
and rollicked away.

Blue

In the white chill of space
a trumpet surge of blue
bursts clear of any shape
swells from paper limbo.

Reflections drift over the glass
shadowy in the pale surround
like statistics, this city's millions of people,
or half heard of ancestors
trailing dust in their dresses,
suddenly bold reaching the heartbeat blue.

They look, frown, finger-curl their hair
tilt their heads to laugh.
Eyes reflect into the depths of paint
from a blue that is distance, not surface.

They pass on, tread into the border, fade.

I hold tight,
my own reflection fierce with stillness
unwilling to move till the guard stalks me down.

Abstracts

1

The mind will not be stilled
by a numb expanse
white below pitch,
will travel, roam about until it reaches

darkness
blind beyond the horizon
on the edge of another planet

but in the heave of soft snow
something of ours.
Shapes within snow
not an ear or lily or thorns or a donkey's jaw
but brushstrokes
textures of the brush pushing around
making no claims, only,
we make everything.

And the rim of the world is not quite sheer
cilia of paint pulsing there
into the dark.

2

Newborn

feathered in lace
rolled in purplish black like a bruise
and the drift of air all round is grey
a passing thought

though the reproduction
fixes it as solid brown.

3

Whether you go through or not
it arches there
flame soft as down
blooming from a deeper red that sinks away
like unseen blood at the back of your eyes.

Burning softly all around you
whether you sit numb on the cushioned bench
or slip over the shining floor to the exit.

4

Purple vapour
barely lifting from space

smoke fringed
a book floating open
hazy, may drift away
or a two-winged gateway
trace only

breath on cold air

no reproduction.

Hints

'Roam the unknown.'
I'm not good at getting lost,
crave a story-book trail of peas
etched by rodent teeth, mushed by hooves.
Crook my head backwards
note the stile, the forked trunk
shred of black plastic whistling on a twig.
It will look like this on the way back
marked by queer outcroppings.
This is how it'll look.

But it doesn't.
I return soon from what might have been
the tipping, open rim of things
had I not taken care to punctuate
each slithering step, wedging it in a familiar mould
so there's no unknown to reach.
Returning there are no signs
no singling out of meaning.
The way back is normal as breathing,
a quiet, rutted track.

'Call things by their proper names.'
I poke about in a mesh of whispers –
nothing beyond but wily cloud
loud swarms of others' meanings.
I pluck a shiny globe ripened out of spikes
cup it tender in my palm
and utter –
it dulls, dead wood.
I glimpse a muscled being hurtle across the track
something given-up clenched in its jaws.
It stops, turns, glares
giving me a last chance and I utter –
it lopes into cartoon.
I try and try and utter wee wee wee all the way home.

'Write the world into existence.'
I sink into the sofa
weep for nothing,
fill with my tears a bowl for a circling fish
and write with my fingers in the air.

Testimony

Coming from an empty corral in the desert
holding someone's hand
you'll never know who
never name with your pen or explain
or find again, filling the endless sky.

Only tell how desert flowers
prick up from the sand.

Through Silence

When a sunset makes no demand
to be syllabled into glory
– enough to say to a friend, Look!
    and turn home

when shadows don't script the forest floor
with signs for crafted telling
– they flop, underside of light and wind
    dulling into dark

when to answer birdsong with words
doesn't complete the world's making
– is merely a neighbourly nod in passing
    to a busy bird

will life have voice enough?
– a leaf flapping in the shade
    or an old poet, hands deep in her pockets
    moving her lips in silence.

The Fearful Poet

Clutch against dispersal,
strain to hear the trumpet call through fog,
scratch among long grasses – call them 'whispering' –
and green stones, for the grimace of the plaster leprechaun.
Click the gate shut according to the Country Code,
live in a house in a street called Laurel
among poems framed like certificates.
Don't speak among people
for fear they'll mess up your ideas.

The Poet and Beatrice

Face down, the poem, hiding what it cannot say
where my mind slurs on death,
can only roar at grandeur, joy,
and words only clip a neat geometry.

'No pictures,' I warn my niece.
She reaches up, grasps the paper
gazes at print.
'*Pretend* there's pictures,' she laughs.
'An elephant eating an olive!'

Gift-horse

Sometimes it speaks to me, mouthing
shapes that flicker as light on choppy waters
this deep-bearded figure from below
swaying in ritual silks
and sometimes gestures softly to an opening door.
But I scowl, grip my pen
ache with the effort
to make sense.

It bows, crawls into the old record player
pulls the doors in on itself.
Clicks them shut,
honey-coloured wood veneer.
And then I only hear the static.

An eyelash may
float onto my blank paper
like a comma, adrift.

Colouring In

She settles them to it
tucking their wriggling bodies
into red and blue overalls
compact as paint squares.
Her gaze holds down their shimmering heads
as she fiddles with her ring
lets her hand flutter over her stomach
pushes aside the newspaper
watching her children
willing them.
As if every shaky outline
could be filled in with blocks of living colour
and the shape made whole.

Next Door

We don't like it next door,
we cough in the silence
and the dog goes howling down the road
distant territories, salt mines, diamond mines.
Once, the Shah of Persia's wife
flew over the two trees on the common
the plump one in need of a hairdo
and the scrawny splintered one.
'How green, your country.' Pins between her teeth.
She didn't see the fluff of feathers left by migrating geese
like tufts of dolls' hair ripped out,
wrinkled bags and syringes.
The child plays in her grandfather's Zimmer frame
and we cough next door.

Neighbour

It always shot shivers through me, Bob's garden,
one rose struggling out of a rectangle of scraped earth,
the nail-clippings of his lawn
in a small mound behind the shed,
and when one day I discovered my tall, air-licking weeds
lying crushed with chemical brown,
their necks broken against the fence,
and saw the can of poison jeering
in the dead centre of his lawn
that's when I decided to grow marrows in my front garden
right on the tight-lipped street.

Let them lie full and brazen with juice
let me stroke their gleaming bellies every morning
let old Bob avert his pebble eyes
as he grumbles out into the street
to buy cigarettes and complain to the neighbours.
Let the marrows lie plump on the crest of the rich earth
in my front garden.
Also I thought, maybe a rude flowering of rhubarb...

All summer I lay in the sun dreaming of this,
topless, sunning my winter breasts like bulbs dug up too early,
but before I had the chance, Bob's garden grew ragged.
There was a sprouting in the roof gutters.
His car port was empty.
Then his son and grandchildren came, took a few things away,
and a red FOR SALE notice planted itself
in his careful front garden.

Other

I left a boy in the woods once
– should I regret? –
a boy prancing over beechnuts and droppings
swiping the trees with a stick
his head lost in a helmet
huge as a brass chamber pot.
Or did I see his tongue
caught elfin between his teeth
and did I almost put my mouth around
his creamy arms
or touch his bare tummy
before I turned?
It was his legs, rearing up
bulging like pine cones
and furred with some foul, shaggy stuff
scrabbled up from a hole in the earth.
And his split feet
as he veered towards me, blindly.

I remember the wood
a gleam of metal rods, bits of cog-wheel
claptrap and props stuffed
in the fork of a sour tree,
the heave and clatter of that wood
– not even a forest it seemed to me then
just a dense copse.
I left him to his play.

I floated off, knowing my dress sinuous, soft
a second, calmer skin
the folds pooling blue into air.
Long, lissom years then
plaiting the golden braids of my hair
into the golden braids of my dress
fastening my brooch of cool grey pebbles
a moonstone at the heart,
between my breasts like a pale rose window.

Years dreaming through the long, intelligent bones of my hands
as I write my words on the mirror
in reverse script
so my reflection may read.

I remember a pale green land beyond the wood,
hints of blue mountains
where some day I may find
a hollow rock with a virgin and child.

But I only remember the boy
when my feet arch,
flow hot, writhe
at the hem of my dress.

Untitled 1

On the white numb reaches of endless snow
scurry a few bright-patched organisms,
people and running animals.

There is nothing else
to love.

Not a Warm Person

'I'm always cold inside.'
Huddling under layers while the sun blazed
indifferent, outside.
'You need children,' the doctor said.

Not long after,
my fingers started swelling, puffing up like ruddy sausages
a great roaring inside
and my chest, my stomach area –
if I was dead you'd call it my torso –
which usually felt like the inside of a fridge
with the light off
grew, heat rounding in me, pushing at my tight ribs
so for a minute my breath was trapped until they softened
into warm plasticene
and I swelled, a huge rosy watermelon
soaked in alcohol not water
and all the while this heat was throbbing inside, pushing
at the skin of my arms and legs, a furry animal
nudging its way through my veins,
and I stood, to claim this great being,
had to heave myself up with the crooked stick at my side
which slipped itself into my grasp
and as I stood I saw how outside the sky was a grey sheen.
Prickles danced through the skin on my cheeks and chin
and a mass of white hairs flowered like hoarfrost
like crystals from nothing
softening as it grew to baby down, to the soft white fur
we found on winter hedges when I was a child.
And suddenly I was striding round the room in a berry-red coat
which reached down to my proud boots and swung,
trimmed with white fur, and I was gathering
from behind the sofa, the mantelpiece
the corners of the cupboard,
coloured packages
parcels of all the shapes in the world.

I stood at the steamed-up window
looking at the chimneys and tower blocks of London,
thinking about the dust and tight walls,
the shaky balconies, the air shafts and rubbish chutes
to get to all the tossing and turning and gentle sleep
of the children.
I opened the window, clambered onto the ledge
felt the first snowflakes melt on my nose
and knew at last the cold was on the outside.

'Do you put smiling faces on your suns?'

In a country where the sheep eat garlic
I find myself alive
and far from home.

In a country where spouting volcanoes
juggle stones round as melons
tumbling them onto little red roofs
and the sheep laugh in their bellies

I turn somersaults.

Where the skeletons dance,
proud spiky fingers reaching out
and each has three pairs of ribs
exact as an I-Ching sign

I walk on stilts.

And where the children zigzag
giggling through jungle colours
I try not to think of home
and the pitfalls of breath.

Woolwich River Walk

These grey waters drifting into the horizon
and fat old floats, turning
slow in the water,
and the man at the end of the path, hanging over the railing
with no need
to turn and glance at me.

I come here sometimes
came here first when I needed time to flow on
to forget a loss, common enough
shrieking.
And I needed this steady path by old sludge River Thames
to be like the candyfloss walkway on New York's brisk river
my first place of recovery;
arch, rattling city, consumed with its own
different life
and achieved home of my oldest friend.
Bricklaid pathways, pink, there and here,
though here the moss is already growing in streaks
like damp patches
and there are no smug period shops perched on the jetties
no souvenirs.

And I needed to remember too the sullen Greenwich water-bus
a time before the time before,
one pale afternoon with my oldest friend
knowing she'd soon break loose for America. Emigrate.
We slid embalmed
through colourless river air and the brush of water
and only river-sour smells and the mocking grace of bird droppings
and gulls wheeling as they must
angling in the silken damp and rocking air
at home with movement,
and the way down river always opening to a white sky.
We sat in silence knowing it would happen.

And I thought then, yes, perhaps travel
time and space is all right after all
not a smashing of one's life
but rather a gentle extension
space for one to live.
And the wheelings and shiftings of who may be dear
and here, at any one time,
not schism but how it is.

Yesterday there was a boy fishing down on the churned-up sand
his bike propped against the river wall.
Another bike lay in the water
water slapping over its wheels.

Sand Dollar

Fragile this bone-white shell
and is it 'dollar' or 'dolour'?
Just a disc of calcium pricked into lace,
you could crunch it, an easy accident.
A five-petalled star in the centre
and in a slow circle-dance around the rim,
six careful slits, slender as wands.
Dwelling for tongue-soft life
under the drift of sea.

Hard to search out a sand dollar
under the hum of sea, under the ocean bed
just a slight patterning of the sand,
nearly missed
like a trace.

For Margaret

Speaking the Wetlands

It doesn't ask to be spoken, this place,
pools of light gleaming ragged in age-brown marshes
stretching further than vision
under the sweep of slow white sky,
though I stand here on lifting turf
with my clutch of language, in my red anorak,
choked with the wanting
to name, to claim in incantation
the meander of long water slipping
curling through rounded brown clay,
silence but for the call of birds and the flapping and rising
out of the tough-sprung growths of the marsh,
birds streaked black and white gathering, wheeling
getting on with their life
and the roar of the sea far away.
It just is.
Only pointed birds' feet markings
picked over the wide mud
wander like trails of tiny arrows.

It doesn't ask to be spoken
this merging of the shades of sleep, browns and greys
just an age-staining of air, water,
birdsong following flight over the pale arc of sky.

It doesn't ask to be spoken though my mind gibbers
wanting to word into sacrament
the light, the slow turning of clay
and water's flow.
I wait, restless on the dyke, lips chilled,
wanting to speak it

wanting it to speak to me.

In a wash of pale sunlight
the little clawprints ripple
crisscrossing over the mud,
quick, elusive strands of DNA
weaving into life

and my heart beats and my skin hums.

Buddleia

Buddleia attracts butterflies,
not angels.

See how
every uncurling purple floret
shelters a five-tipped star
pink as a baby's fingernails,
how it smells so heady, amazing – dear
as the world God saw was good.

And how it dangles over war-ripped houses,
rustling camouflage shadows
on dark stained walls, attracting butterflies,
continues its merry purple bobbing in the field
where a child lies screaming under the weight of a man.

Just as the sun rose again over Hiroshima
though there was no one to cast a shadow.

Standing Stones

Only their circling is familiar,
each stone intent as the back of a priest.

You press your hand against the rough surface
neither hot nor cold, no more than a thought is.
You run your finger along the mean cracks
as if to conjure something harboured in ancient stone,
as if there were some answer
in the dawn-of-time
not the beginning of the question
ravelling like sheep's wool on barbed wire,
this anxious spiralling of carbon, to where?
The stone is still as bone.
No humming into your palm.

Sheep tear steadily at the grass
knowing what they're about.

You read, there is a history.

While Newton mapped the mechanics of the universe
local churchmen grew troubled by village mutterings,
a queer-limbed creature howling in a knot behind the hedge,
the way the stone shadows on certain days
slid finely to the clip of the moon's rising
as if dark seals were set in sunlight,
marked by the stones,
an expectancy.

The churchmen dug deep
crammed straw around the stones' roots,
struck fire, bellowed flames
to burn and crack them out of joint.
With hammers, ropes, knives,
they tumbled and fractured the stones.

Villagers lugged away the smaller blocks
to plug their homes
against wind and the cawing of rooks.
The stones lay felled.
Year by year grass grew over, making soft mounds
as if household pets were buried there.

Resurrected now, the circle's complete,
only the cracks hinting.

Rock, North America

You remember no dream
except you told knuckle bones
in its jagged shadow
Safeways broad over the water
two fling cameras for the price of one.

The rock's high canyons gripped
a hollow place, blank to the sky
where a red cardinal's wing was broken.
Someone scuffed the soil
then moved away with the grainy wind of evening.

You took seven photos of the rock
remember no prophecy.

Self-help

One grumpy morning
I bought myself a bunch of daffodils
bright as toys.
No one to buy flowers for me
but the universe has gifted them
says the helpful rainbow-streaked paperback.

So there they lift.
Still, glowing trumpets
lit by my anglepoise.
Amazing and they know it,
positive-thinking daffodils.

This Far

Square upon square of glass banked up
beyond the ache of our craning,
towers like walls upended
– stood suddenly upright, as we once –
blocking against whatever is not us,
and aeroplanes laying cool claim
to fragments of sky.

On the sidewalk a girl in trainers
flexes her legs up behind her
pelican-like
to be sure of muscle, of flesh

and caught in a cleft the round sun
flares, splinters glass edges
a fist springing open.

City Signs

Stark this heat, original.
I scowl at what should be a crowning sky
and shiver that the paving stones are blank
as if something's worn away.

People's graffiti shadows strut, writhe, shrivel.
'Nietzsche is dead – God'
scrawled somewhere in the Underground.

In the park the paths swing round and round
like a circus act.
The grass is smeared with bits of shade
pigeons push past the fat knotting of lovers
and in and out of clattering gates all down the street
a child in frilled white socks delivers a leaflet.
A street party; there'll be dancing, bravado,
people weaving hot music into the night.

Should I tangle in this flesh sticky All
or kneel somewhere, gaping at a cut-out moon?

Untitled 2

Leaves glimmering
silvery flames votive
to an absolute sky
and trunk rooted in a time
when, perhaps, people knew.

I want to fold and kneel

can only wait

letting the sun lie warm
as an arm on my shoulders,
gazing at this one
shining olive tree.

Signs on the Way

In a car with bullbars I coast into shadows
driving away from those who pray.

Snow mulched now into fleshy earth
woodsmoke furs the air
sunlight springing clear,
a hawk hovers in the open sky
and I drive into the forest

where shadow branches web the ground
veining the way,
– strokes of an unknown script
a map of the hidden city
or wing-prints of light
cast through church windows –
glimpses from a dream I'm leaving
wavering in my mind's shadow.

I drive
dark-light brushing through me
nudging thoughts I don't know how to think
– lurch forward, flick on the radio –
invitations to virtual reality
the latest on the blither show
relativism, freedom – get a life –
get real, the labyrinth is our home –
this manic play of life articulating air.

In the mirror the shadows lie in ruins.
And where's the sign for Route 666
sign of the Beast?
I swing the car onto the broad-backed freeway
and head on.

Journey on the Edge

Against bare brown trees hung
with torn branches and grey shreds of growth,
against the ache of a clearing,
one woodframe house, a tricycle perhaps, a car,
against brown forests shouldering over the heave of hills
and villages scattered white along the road,
winter-beaten lawns merged between each neat home
and only a church pitting its cemetery against dry trees
no school, no shop, bare habitation,
against the scraggy shadow of the wind
the motel woman has hung in her window
a garland of pink plastic
shaped like a heart
and at night I, city dweller, dream

a glowing grass terrace, a high ledge
sheer above a lake.
A smiling peasant woman in myth-bright costume
kneels, resilient, to work the terrace
glances up at the sun,
while far below a man wades deep into the water
a man brown and ordinary
like someone fishing on a quiet Sunday
– and now the lake is not so far down
or it's rising gently, swelling, murky…
I don't know how to hold taut the tension
this vital distance
between the woman on the edge, cultivating,
and the man wading into the deep brown flood.

Morning stirs me with the smell of hash browns
and on the radio there's Elvis Presley
who had golden taps in the home where he died.

In Winter

Times I turn airwards, away
skimming this sweep of sand
sea-rippled shore
limpid sea so far it could be sky
all long as a bird's wing

this reach of space, clear
shows up the knots and junk
slithering over my eyes
graffiti I gaze through

to draw in deep
the drift of shore easing into air
bathe and clear my vision

but always people, bobbling the far sands
lumpy, as if trudging home from work
trouble this wide flow

though as they come close their faces glow
like little moons
catching the winter sun.

Mark

When I'm old, and the time gone

will I remember how this baby
moves a crayon over paper, pauses
to see it's her bright touch
has changed the space?

Sea, sky

Not murky this haze
no more than the blur of galaxies,
this seaport in blue dusk
the crane's thin scratch
furred over
towers fading in sky, sea,
sea vapour drifting into sky
all one reach of luminous blue-grey mist

only, somewhere
claggy earth may be distinct
and whiskery grasses

our ground,
the world's minor portion.

Search

This should be the place, dust and ancient heat,
but only toothless bell-towers crack the sky,
roofs curled tight as bound feet, hooded shadows
circling, sweeping husks from the ragged ground.
I cut my finger on a holy book,
the blood pooled and blanched in the dragon heat.
Then you came. Your hair smelled of rain and fruit.
Though you led me up the sacred mountain
tearing at thorns to show me tablets of stone
humming with hieroglyphics, and although
the sunset looped a halo round the world's peaks
and a tortoise wrote slowly in the dust
I thought, it's nothing, will be nothing,
till we lie close, like hands folded in prayer.

Original

Lay the soles of your feet bare,
hushed on this warm red earth.
Crouch, and round it rich in your palms
as if you were moulding a child.
Tread softly on this sacred land.

A quick nudge at your ankle –
wrinkled, low-bellied – gone
scattering stones into a crackle of thistles,
no bones about making a noise!

This Side of Paradise

If there are angels I hope
their wings, triangular, exact and lifting light
will be sharp as harriers screaming overhead.

I hope they'll be lithe, muscular
prancing and dancing in the air, mock-punching
catching at each other's floating robes,
bouncing toddlers,
or drifting away alone, robes draughty,
or curling into silence.

I hope they'll be secretive, inward
old as the cactus popping with spiked succulence.

I need to know
I am not an aberration.

Perhaps

It's the life of the elderly woman in the anorak
bending over her dog in the dewy park,
of heavy crows hopping and stopping on the glimmering grass
pecking over the lines where the blades are whited stiff,
of litter fluttering in the long, numb shadows.
The life you have to unearth for yourself
and hold in cupped hands, like an egg
or like air.

Something There Is

A rag rug in an aunt's spare room
empty spaces between the furniture

jumble-sale colours
weaving warm under the bones of your feet
where you happen to be on a patch of ground
in a white universe.

Trick

Dozing on a heat-stunned shore
veer awake –

light laid bare
sheering into dips, bends

light inlaid with light

till wisps of shadow – wily
round into humps of things
rocks, bones.

And Left on the Shore

A bleached olive branch
the grain of the wood
skewered
straining about and about
its unclenched twigs,
agony or just growth.

Something missing

as if thoughts were paltry
sideways things

misquotes
of the word that ghosts

leaves us incomplete.

?

Perhaps it will show itself
different
the shock of a negative
light in alien places
dark where we hadn't known it

stark with what we've forgotten.

Sealed

She found it when she was young,
couched in wet grass
under a tree which had brooded there all night
and oozed out a ripple of fungi in the early morning.
Not knowing what she was doing
she slipped it over her wrist,
the knotted cord dangling
the leather box etched with diagonals
– kisses or blessings or crossroads or knives –
the box which had no opening
so she could never know what trick or treasure
it concealed, if anything –
and she skipped off into her long life.